We Live in Nigeria

Donna Bailey and Anna Sproule

M
MACMILLAN

Hello. My name is Mallam and
this is my friend Bala.

We both live in Kano.
Kano is a large city in Northern Nigeria.
It is a very old city.
The oldest part has a big wall around it.

The wall and many of the houses are made of mud bricks which have been baked in the sun.
When the rains come, parts of the walls get washed away.
Then they have to be mended with more mud bricks.

Our house is just inside the walls.
It is a large house with
four compounds inside it.
A compound is like a separate house
inside the main house.

My father and uncles live in one compound.
Mum and the other women don't live in
the same compound as the men.
They live with their children each in
their own compound.

It is very hot and dry in Northern Nigeria.
People often use camels to carry their goods.
These camels are resting in
the lorry park in Kano.
The men are resting in the shade!

The men in Kano wear long loose robes
to keep them cool.
Some robes have beautiful embroidery on them.
Other robes are dyed bright colours.

Some of the cloth for the robes is dyed
in the Kano dye pits.
The men tie and dye the cloth
a deep indigo blue to make
different blue and white patterns.

When the cloth has been dyed, the men use wooden mallets to hammer it smooth.
Then they sell the dyed cloth in the market.

This man has made lots of pots
to sell in the market.
He also sells them from a stall by the road.
Can you see the different patterns
on his pots?

This man sells kebabs from a stall
by the side of the road.
He puts bits of meat on wooden sticks.
He cooks the kebabs on the fire
behind his stall.
His kebabs taste delicious!

Friday is a very important day
in Northern Nigeria.
On Friday everybody goes to the mosque
to say special prayers.

There is a large open space outside the mosque in Kano.
My father and I join the other men and boys.
We take our prayer mats with us and stand in lines facing the mosque.

When we say our prayers, we take off
our shoes and kneel on our mats.
We bow our heads to the ground to pray.

Mum and the women do not pray with the men.
They pray in a separate part of
the mosque which is just for them.

The most important man in Kano is the Emir.
He leads the people in their prayers
inside the mosque.
The Emir lives in a palace near the mosque.
Our picture shows the entrance
to his palace.

Twice a year in Kano there are festivals with a big parade.
They are called Sallah festivals.
Everybody wears their best clothes and goes to watch the parade.

All the important chiefs come to Kano
to join in the parade.
They wear their best robes and
their horses are beautifully decorated.

Early in the morning the Emir of Kano
rides out from his palace.
He is surrounded by his guards and
his most important guests.

The Emir rides to the large open ground
in front of the mosque.
Crowds of people watch him ride past.

In front of the mosque, the Emir and his guards say prayers.

Then the Emir returns to his palace
to watch the parade.

First the musicians parade past the Emir. Some blow horns and others blow trumpets. The drummers bang their drums and make a cheerful noise.

Other musicians ride camels.
Can you see their big drums on
either side of their camels?

The chiefs follow the musicians.
They ride their horses past the Emir
and salute him.

Now the Emir's soldiers come to salute him. The spearmen ride up to the Emir and present their spears to him.

Then comes the charge of the horsemen.
They race their horses up to the Emir and stop only about a metre away from him.
They wave their swords in his face.

After the celebrations drummers
walk around the crowd and entertain them.

There are other entertainments too.
This little girl shows the crowd
her pet snake.

This man has a hyena which
he shows the crowd.
The people keep well away from him!

Soon it is time to go back home.
The people leave the parade ground and walk home.
They are tired and happy after an exciting Sallah festival.

Reading consultant: Diana Bentley
Editorial consultant: Donna Bailey

Illustrated by Sue Barclay/John Martin and Artists Ltd
Picture research by Suzanne Williams
Designed by Richard Garratt Design

First published 1989

Published by
Macmillan Children's Books,
a division of Macmillan Publishers Limited
4 Little Essex Street, London WC2R 3LF and Basingstoke
Associated companies around the world.

Printed in Hong Kong

British Library Cataloguing in Publication Data
Bailey, Donna
We live in Nigeria
1. Nigeria. Social life
I. Title II. Sproule, Anna
III. Series
966.9'05

ISBN 0-333-48676-5

Photographs:
Cover: Rex Parry
Robert Harding Picture Library: 3, 7, 9 and 10
The Hutchison Library: 6 (Chandana Juliet Highet), 12, 13, 14, 15, 16, 20, 21, 24 and 28
Rex Parry: 2, 8, 11, 17, 18, 19, 25, 27, 29, 30, 31 and 32
Rex Features: 26
ZEFA: 1